TITUS:
LIFE-CHANGING TRUTH
IN A WORLD OF LIES

Jeff Dodge

STUDY GUIDE WITH LEADER'S NOTES

New
Growth
Press
newgrowthpress.com

New Growth Press, Greensboro, NC 27401
newgrowthpress.com
Copyright © 2020 by Jeff Dodge

Cover Design: Faceout Books, faceoutstudio.com
Interior Design and Typesetting: Gretchen Logterman
Exercises and Application Questions: Jack Klumpenhower

ISBN: 978-1-64507-073-3 (Print)
ISBN: 978-1-64507-089-4 (eBook)

Printed in India

28 27 26 25 24 23 22 21   2 3 4 5 6

CONTENTS

INTRODUCTION

Titus is a letter from one missionary to another. As such, we would expect it to be full of the gospel. After all, gospel truth is what missionaries proclaim. Their purpose is to tell the wonder-filled good news of all Jesus is and all he gives to those who believe in him, and to see his kingdom expand.

So, it should be no surprise that as you study the book of Titus you will learn about the gospel—or "knowledge of the truth," as it is put in the very first sentence. What might surprise you, though, is the rich variety of uses for this gospel truth that pop up in this brief letter. It turns out that gospel truth isn't just about soul winning and church planting. It's also about soul refining and church growing. It's about courageous leadership and faithful following. It's about purity, respect, love, humility, devotion to family, trustworthiness at work, and support for the church's great mission. The gospel powers the whole Christian life.

Like the other small-group resources in this series, this book will show you those connections between the truth of the gospel and a godly life. You will consider how the good news of Jesus propels you out, on mission, to love and serve others. And you will practice returning to the gospel daily, for comfort and renewed hope, when life on mission gets hard.

HOW TO USE THIS STUDY

This guide will help you do this in a group study. Titus was written to a leader in the church, and it is meant to strengthen every member of that church body. Studying with other Christ followers lets you benefit from what God is also teaching them, and it gives you encouragement and accountability as you apply what you learn.

Gospel-centered growth includes growing in awareness of your sin and in confidence that Jesus saves you in every way from that sin. Therefore, the group will be a place to share not only successes, but also sins and needs. Expect differences in how God is working in each group participant. Also expect differences in how people join in. It's okay if some in the group are cheery while others are weary, if some "get it" quickly while others want to look more deeply, or if some are eager to share while others take it slowly. But because you'll be studying the Bible and praying together, also expect the Holy Spirit to work. Expect people to grow and to become "eager to do good works" (Titus 2:14). And expect that to start with you!

Each participant should have one of these study guides in order to join in reading and be able to work through the exercises during that part of the study. The study leader should read through both the lesson and the leader's notes in the back of this book before each lesson begins. Otherwise, no preparation or homework is required from any participant.

There are seven lessons in this study guide. Each lesson will take about an hour to complete, perhaps a bit more if your group is large, and will include these elements:

BIG IDEA. This is a summary of the main point of the lesson.

BIBLE CONVERSATION. You will read a passage from Titus and discuss it. As the heading suggests, the Bible conversation questions are intended to spark a conversation rather than generate correct answers. In most cases, the questions will have several possible good answers and a few best answers. The leader's notes at the back of this book provide some insights, but don't just turn there for the "right answer." At times you may want to see what the notes say, but always try to answer for yourself first by thinking about the Bible passage.

ARTICLE. This is the main teaching section of the lesson, written by the book's author.

DISCUSSION. The discussion questions following the article will help you apply the teaching to your life. Again, there will be several good ways to answer each question.

EXERCISE. The exercise is a section you will complete on your own during group time. You can write in the book if that helps you, or you can just think about your responses. You will then share some of what you learned with the group. If the group is large, it may help to split up to share the results of the exercise and to pray, so that everyone has a better opportunity to participate.

WRAP-UP AND PRAYER. Prayer is a critical part of the lesson because your spiritual growth will happen through God's work in you, not by your self-effort. You will be asking him to do that good work.

Titus will show you how gospel truth is anything but static. If you are a follower of Jesus, it is active and alive in you. It leads to godliness (1:1) and makes you ready for every good work (3:1). If you have ever doubted its power in you, now is the time to look more deeply at the love of Christ proclaimed in this short book of the Bible, and let its truth transform you.

1

TRUTH THAT LEADS TO GODLINESS

BIG IDEA

God's truth is a powerful treasure. We should pay close attention and expect it to change us, leading to godliness.

BIBLE CONVERSATION *15 MINUTES*

The book of Titus is a letter from the missionary Paul to his close associate and fellow missionary, Titus. In addition to this letter, Paul also mentions working alongside Titus in 2 Corinthians, Galatians, and 2 Timothy, suggesting that Titus was well-traveled and familiar with Paul's ministry. The occasion for this letter is that Paul had left Titus on the Mediterranean island of Crete to build up recently-planted churches there, where immorality was part of the island's reputation and false teachers were already springing up among God's people.

Begin your study of Titus by having someone read **Titus 1:1–4** aloud. Then discuss the questions below as a group.

Paul describes himself as God's servant and as an *apostle*, which means "one sent on a mission." List the purposes behind Paul's service and mission. Which purpose most makes you want to read the rest of his letter, and why?

"Knowledge of the truth that leads to godliness"

"hope of eternal life"

Based on Paul's purposes, how can you expect the rest of his letter to help someone who is engaged in mission? Which of these helps do you most need in your life, and why?

Both

Need to rest more in His hope

Paul takes pains to say not only that he is a servant of God and an apostle, but also that his preaching is commanded by God and contains God's revelation. How should reading his words be different from listening to an everyday believer? How might it affect the way you study Titus?

Paul's words are essentially God's words, not interpreted words passed on to us.

Now read the following article by this book's author. Take turns reading it aloud for the benefit of the whole group, switching readers at the paragraph breaks. Then discuss the questions at the end of the article.

Lesson

ARTICLE

WORDS FROM GOD

5 MINUTES

Introductions are important. As we begin our journey through a new book of the Bible, these first words must never be skipped or read too quickly.

First-century letters were treasures. The paper and the utensils were precious commodities. If you had the opportunity to write a letter, you weighed every word. Even the introductory words were very intentional. Those opening lines spoke volumes. They set a tone. They revealed something important about both the author and the recipients. Here you often discover the purpose for writing and the heartbeat of the message to follow. There is a lot to be gained as we mine just four verses.

As Titus unrolled this letter he was met with the familiar (perhaps less-than-perfect) penmanship of his mentor and friend. Titus's heart must have been warmed as he noted that Paul referred to himself first as a "servant of God" and then as an "apostle of Jesus Christ."

Paul was carrying on a sacred tradition and passing it on to Titus. Like Abraham, Moses, Joshua, and especially Jesus, the title *servant of God* was worn as a badge of honor. It spoke of the humility that was to mark leaders among God's people. It also points to the proper positioning of leaders before the throne of the Most High.

Additionally, Paul was an *apostle*. He was sent by God to represent Jesus Christ. Paul was bringing more than words from a friend; he was writing authoritative words from God. Note that Paul even refers to his preaching as something entrusted to him "by the command of God our Savior." This letter to warm Titus's heart was also to call him to attention.

This means that as we read the book of Titus, we need to lean in is as if a trusted mentor is writing to us. But we must also have a deep respect for the real Author—God, our Father who is also the King of all creation. Because he is our Master, he tells us what a proper response to his words looks like: "I will look favorably on this kind of person: one who is humble, submissive in spirit, and trembles at my word" (Isaiah 66:2). These words are for our good and our joy, but they are not to be trifled with. They are to be obeyed, because they are from God—the same God who created us, loves us, redeems us, and is transforming us into the very likeness of Jesus.

This letter is addressed to God's elect—to Christ followers, saved by Jesus and regenerated (made new) by the Holy Spirit. And then comes these riveting words: "knowledge of the truth that leads to godliness." We have not even made it past the first verse and already a phrase that is pregnant with meaning has hit us. Now do you see why we can't fly through the introduction too quickly? This is the theme of Titus, the banner under which Paul is writing this important letter.

Truth. Titus lives on an island known for its lies and its liars (see 1:12). But now God, who cannot lie and will not lie, is bringing truth to Crete. And this truth is not meant to sit on a shelf to be admired. It is not simply a weapon to win arguments. Truth is not static and it certainly is not stagnant. It does more than set the record straight. Truth bursts on the scene and changes everything. Truth leads to godliness.

People in our modern Western world often fall into the trap of imagining a life in which it is perfectly rational to believe or think one way but make decisions and actually live in a way that stands in contrast to their belief. For instance, it is not uncommon in our culture for someone to identify themselves with a religion (Christianity, Islam, Judaism, etc.) but not actually hold to the stated tenets of that religion or practice a lifestyle that accords with that religion. They see no contradiction here. In fact, they may be offended if you say, "But how can you say you are a _____ (Christian/Muslim/Jew) when you openly disagree with what _____ (Christianity/Islam/Judaism) teaches and you don't actually live according to those principles?

This ability to divide belief from action is a relatively new way of thinking on the world stage. More, it runs counter to the way God designed us to think and live. Those who are elect, who have experienced the kindness of God in salvation (3:4), who have been born again by the Holy Spirit (3:5), are people whose beliefs correspond to a new way of life. Scripture transforms us from the inside out, precisely because it is God's true Word given to us as his beloved children. Truth leads to godliness.

Be warned: there are people who think differently about this. The end of chapter 1 mentions some who claim to know God but deny him by their works. This letter reminds Titus, and each of us who reads these words, that there is to be a necessary connection between belief in God's truth and a changed life. The new trajectory of our life is to point toward godliness.

This is a small letter, but don't be fooled by its brevity. It packs a punch. We must not approach this study simply as a means of growing in our knowledge of the truth. We must prepare to be changed. In fact, when we hear the words of God, we *must change* in response.

Titus is a true son to Paul. Paul loves Titus with a passionate, fatherly love. And he is entrusting Titus with a monumental task—establishing a beachhead for the church on the notorious island of Crete. Scary stuff. But Titus is not alone. Jesus is with him. And these words from Paul will be a tremendous help to guide him. May they be so for us as well!

DISCUSSION *10 MINUTES*

Think about "knowledge of the truth that leads to godliness." Tell about a time when you learned some truth from the Bible and you become godlier as a result. Or share about a time when you learned new truth but resisted changing.

Much Bible truth does not tell us directly how to live, but instead gives us good news. For example, verse 2 mentions "the hope of eternal life that God, who cannot lie, promised before time began." How might that kind of good-news truth change how you live? Give a specific example from your life, if you can.

Lesson

EXERCISE

THE SWORD OF GOD'S WORD

20 MINUTES

As we think about listening to God's truth, you may recall that the Bible pictures the word of God as a sword. Hebrews 4:12–13 says, "For the word of God is living and effective and sharper than any double-edged sword, penetrating as far as the separation of soul and spirit, joints and marrow. It is able to judge the thoughts and intentions of the heart. No creature is hidden from him, but all things are naked and exposed to the eyes of him to whom we must give an account."

In that passage, the sword is not used by us in battle but rather is used by God for surgery. His word exposes us and gets into every joint of our person, so that we cannot hide and must instead let it change us.

For this exercise, consider how you tend to treat God's Word, the Bible. What kind of sword is it to you? Begin by working on your own: read through the descriptions below and note some that are most true of you. Try to be honest even though some might be bad ways you use the Bible and others, while valid, are not the best way to use the Bible. When the group is ready, you'll have a chance to share and discuss some of your responses.

I tend to treat God's Word as . . .

. . . a sword on the shelf. I admire it and look at it often, but I seldom take it down and really use it in my life.

❐ I like to learn more of God's Word because it feels good to have Bible knowledge.

❐ I more often quote the Bible to repeat my favorite verses, not to challenge myself with hard verses.

. . . an ornamental sword. I wear it to dress myself up and look good, but I don't sharpen it lest it prick me.

❐ I like to learn more of God's Word because people expect me to know it or admire me for it.

❐ I more often quote the Bible to sound spiritual, not to actually become more spiritual.

. . . a sword pointed at others. I take it out for battle against those who disagree with me.

❐ I like to learn more of God's Word so I can win spiritual arguments.

❐ I more often quote the Bible to correct and direct others, not to correct and direct myself.

. . . a sword pointed at myself. I see it first of all as God's sword, wielded by him to expose and shape me.

❐ I like to learn more of God's Word because it helps me trust Jesus, repent of my sin, and go out into the world with love for others.

❏ I more often quote the Bible privately, to myself, because I need its corrections and gospel promises daily.

The Word of God is again called a sword in Ephesians 6:17. There, it is part of the armor we use to resist the devil's schemes by covering ourselves in the gospel—the truth, righteousness, salvation, etc. we have in Jesus. So finish the exercise by completing the sentence below.

I am willing to let God's Word expose and shape me because it also assures me that Jesus gives me _____
_____.

When the group is ready, share some of your responses. How do you tend to use the Bible, and why? What changes would you like to make?

What gospel blessing did you put in the blank at the end of the exercise? How does it encourage you to let God expose your life and change it?

WRAP-UP AND PRAYER *10 MINUTES*

As part of your closing prayer time together, ask God to be a skillful surgeon during your study of Titus, exposing you where necessary while he also speaks the gospel to you. Also pray that you would accept the teaching of his Word.

2

TRUTH AND LEADERSHIP

BIG IDEA

God trains and protects us by giving us good leaders who show us how to live blamelessly. We each have a role in this pattern of godly growth.

BIBLE CONVERSATION *15 MINUTES*

Having greeted Titus and reminded him of the glorious ministry they share, Paul's first instruction is to make sure Titus gets to the important work of appointing elders in the new churches on Crete. Have someone read **Titus 1:5–14** aloud. (Verses 10 through 14 will be examined more thoroughly as part of the next lesson, but it helps to include them here to understand the context.) Then discuss the questions below.

Based on Paul's description of an elder's job and the problems on Crete, what might be some reasons godly elders are necessary for the church? How might Paul respond today to a person who says, "I don't need elders, I just follow Jesus"?

① To shepherd. The flock in Truth; Rebuke Theological lies + protect The Flock.

② That is not biblical. We are called to community

Verses 6 through 9 describe what it looks like for an elder to be blameless (some translations say "above reproach"). Which of the traits listed feel especially needed in your community or culture, and why?

— Held firm to the word so as to give
   instruction in sound doctrine.
There are lots of teachings that are
counter to the truth.

Verse 9 says an elder must both encourage the people with sound teaching and refute wrong teaching. What personal or spiritual qualities might help an elder do both well?

— Lover of good
— not arrogant
— not quick tempered
— Self controlled
— upright / holy [good reputation]

****

Now read this lesson's article aloud, switching readers at each paragraph break. Then discuss the questions at the end of the article.

Lesson

2

ARTICLE

THE PATTERN FOR FOLLOWING CHRIST

5 MINUTES

Titus was commissioned with a clear and vital mission: secure the church in Crete! A beachhead for the gospel was established there. God's people had been brought to faith through the preaching of the good news of Jesus Christ. Now it was imperative that they be brought safely into the community of local churches. Titus was entrusted with this essential task.

Christians are not to drift alone, but are to flourish in the safety and nourishment of the local church. Dutch theologian Herman Bavinck does not overstate it when he writes, "Whoever isolates himself from the church loses the truth of the Christian faith. That person becomes a branch that is torn from the tree and shrivels, an organ that is separated from the body and therefore doomed to die. Only within the communion of the saints can the length and the breadth, the depth and the height, of the love of Christ be comprehended."[1]

The apostle gave Titus (and us!) the most direct way to ensure the establishment and security of local churches: *discover and appoint godly leaders*. Note that there is no instruction here about finding

---

1 Herman Bavinck, *Reformed Dogmatics*, ed. John Bolt, trans. John Vriend (Grand Rapids, MI: Baker Academic, 2008), 1:79.

18

a building for the church to meet in. There is no advice on the style of music that will draw people in. The liturgy goes unmentioned. Paramount to Titus's task is establishing leaders.

If you were tasked with finding leaders for an organization, the most natural thing to ask would be, "Can you tell me what these leaders are to do? Then I can go find the best candidates for the job." But God's church doesn't work like that. Titus is not told what the leaders *do*; he is told who the leaders are to *be*.

Paul is simply passing on to Titus what he had first learned from Jesus—the gospel takes root and transforms people through personal relationships. This "life-on-life" way of spreading the gospel is how Jesus has designed his church to grow. At times it's messy, and it often seems inefficient. But Jesus doesn't follow our playbook, and God's kingdom doesn't conform to human expectations. Jesus is a personal God, who wants a personal relationship with us, and he uses other people to carry out his plan. His ways are above and beyond us. He always knows best.

As the gospel of Jesus Christ begins to permeate the island of Crete, the young believers need to know how this newfound truth actually leads to godliness, as Paul claimed in verse 1. Jesus's plan is not to pass out "how to" guides. Instead, his plan is to put examples of godliness into every church. The elect in every town are to *see* and *hear* godliness lived out in the lives of the elders.

The believers on the island of Crete had a long way to go. Paul says much was "left undone." Things were pretty messed up in those towns. Can you imagine being Titus? It was not immediately obvious how the gospel was to transform this moral and spiritual train wreck. Paul makes it clear. God is going to use leaders. He is going to use fellow sinners who are learning to live by grace in every area of their lives to impact others and help them learn how to live grace-fueled lives for themselves.

The gospel is a people-to-people business. We receive the gospel as one person hears the gospel from another, and the Holy Spirit enables us to believe it. From there, the young believer is initiated into the community of God's people by being baptized by a follower of Christ. That connection to Christ continues as the young believer is taught to follow Christ in everything. Jesus set up this pattern in his Great Commission at the end of Matthew.

We learn by following. Peter says it: elders are to lead by "being examples to the flock" (1 Peter 5:3). The writer of Hebrews says it: "Remember your leaders who have spoken God's word to you. As you carefully observe the outcome of their lives, imitate their faith" (Hebrews 13:7). And Paul says it about himself: "Imitate me, as I also imitate Christ" (1 Corinthians 11:1). That's the pattern. The way to follow Christ is to follow the example of others who are also following Christ and are a little further down the path of learning to live a life of repentance and faith.

Take a deliberate look at the kinds of qualities Paul urges Titus to discover and cultivate in the future group of Cretan elders. From the list, it seems clear that the truth of the gospel was to lead to godliness in some big areas. Do these qualities look eerily familiar when you think about our own time and place? These elders needed to become living examples of what a godly husband and father was to be. Could it be that the home life of the average Cretan was pretty broken? There were character issues like anger, bullying, greed, and selfishness that needed to be addressed. What does it look like to be patient, kind, peace-making, and others-centered? Oh, and how were the young Christ followers to understand the Bible? There are some complicated things in there! They needed elders who would help them *see* solid teaching and *hear* solid teaching—even in the face of false teaching (the topic of our next lesson!).

Titus had a colossal task. It was vital that he succeed. He had to secure the founding of churches all over the island of Crete. Doing so meant appointing elders in every town to show the elect how the truth of the gospel leads to godliness. How does that look in your corner of the world?

DISCUSSION *10 MINUTES*

What more mature believer have you learned from by example? What about their life or leadership made them a great believer to imitate?

Wayne & Carol
Doug & Sue

Where do you fit in the pattern where more experienced believers imitate Christ, and newer believers learn from them to do the same? What would you like God to do in your life to make you a stronger part of that system (to help you learn from others, or to send you out to mentor others)?

Maturity in the qualition of a elder
Desire
Ability

2

OUR PERFECT ELDER

20 MINUTES

Good elders and pastors are a gift from God, but they are not perfect. Our ultimate hope is not to learn from *them*, but that their lives will point us to *Jesus*—our perfect elder, teacher, and example. The gospel allows us to take a deep look at Jesus's example without feeling burdened or discouraged because we know we are forgiven, have his patient help, and will one day be like him. This means we can look at Jesus's example and say, "Wow, I want to live like him!" with joy, confidence, and anticipation.

For this exercise, you will practice admiring Jesus's example. Begin by working on your own, following these steps:

1. Read through the examples below of how Jesus fits descriptions of an elder mentioned in our passage.
2. Pick *one* you want to explore, and read the Bible passage that goes with it.
3. Note some things about Jesus that you admire and would like to be true of you.

When everyone is ready, you'll have a chance to share and discuss some of your responses.

Not Arrogant

Jesus was humble and constantly took the low place, coming to serve and give his life rather than to be served. EXAMPLE: When Jesus and his disciples gathered to eat the Passover and no slave was with them to wash feet, Jesus took that lowly and dirty job upon himself.

READ: John 13:3–15.

Not a Bully

Jesus was especially gentle and giving toward people whom others discounted or used. EXAMPLE: When a blind man Jesus healed got caught in the crossfire between Jesus and the Pharisees, Jesus didn't use him like the Pharisees did, but found him and spoke the gospel to him.

READ: John 9:24–38.

Not Greedy

Jesus gave up the riches of heaven to live among us sparsely, as a poor man. EXAMPLE: Jesus faced the most severe temptation to be greedy that was possible when the devil showed him the splendor of all the kingdoms of the world and offered them in exchange for a moment of worship, but Jesus refused.

READ: Matthew 4:1–11.

Hospitable

Jesus constantly welcomed outcasts, people far from God, and people others would rather ignore or felt were unimportant. EXAMPLE: When Jesus arrived at the temple, he threw out the moneychangers who were disturbing the court where foreigners gathered, allowed the blind and lame to flock to him, and defended shouting children.

READ: Matthew 21:12–17.

Holy

Jesus never strayed from being obedient to God and set apart for the task of dying for our sin. EXAMPLE: Even when mistreated, Jesus did not respond sinfully, and even when faced with suffering, he remained faithful to God.

READ: 1 Peter 2:21–25.

Self-Controlled

Jesus kept his focus on God's faithfulness and lived with the end-game of his kingdom in mind, even when faced with severe temporary trials. EXAMPLE: On trial before the high priest, Jesus resisted defending himself even when lies were told about him, and answered with courage and faith in God's promises when pressed to respond.

READ: Matthew 26:57–68.

Holding Faithfully to Sound Teaching

Jesus called unbelievers to faith and encouraged those around him by teaching deep truths about God. EXAMPLE: When Jesus bluntly taught his disciples about the dangers of wealth, he also patiently guided them through their concerns, encouraged them to trust God, and gave them hope in the bigness of salvation.

READ: Mark 10:23–31.

Refuting False Teachers

Jesus did not allow false teachers to lead his people astray, but spoke up when necessary. EXAMPLE: In his letter to the church in Pergamum, Jesus acknowledged that they were holding on in a difficult city but still spoke a hard-to-handle rebuke against dangerous teaching among them.

READ: Revelation 2:12–17.

Once you've picked an example above and read the Bible passage that goes with it, think of up to three things you notice about Jesus in that passage. Make them things you admire and find wonder in, and are eager to imitate in your own life.

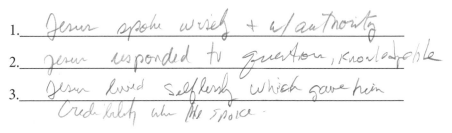

1. _Jesus spoke w/ truth + w/ authority_

2. _Jesus responded to question, Knowledgeable_

3. _Jesus lived selflessly which gave him Credibility when He spoke._

When the group is ready, share some of your responses. Why did you choose them?

When we look at Jesus as our example, we must never forget that he is also our Savior. He forgives us when we fail. He is with us when we struggle. His power in us is what makes us able to be like him. And he will complete his work in us and in the world one day. This means we are freed from making our imitation of Jesus into a burden:

❏ We can imitate Jesus *out of gratitude* rather than to earn his favor.

❏ We can imitate Jesus *out of child-like love* rather than out of slave-like fear.

❏ We can imitate Jesus *joyfully*, as part of a life alongside him rather than a performance for him.

❏ We can imitate Jesus *patiently*, depending on his power and timing as we grow rather than worrying that we haven't progressed far enough yet.

❏ We can imitate Jesus *confidently* rather than giving up because it feels impossible.

❏ We can imitate Jesus *expectantly*, eager to begin today to make ourselves and the world around us fit his coming kingdom.

How might one of these truths change the *way* you work to imitate Jesus? Give an example if you can.

WRAP-UP AND PRAYER *10 MINUTES*

Your imitation of Jesus depends on his work in you. You aren't performing, but relying. So pray for God to help you become more like Jesus in the ways you desire from the exercise.

3

TRUTH, PURITY, AND CHRIST ALONE

BIG IDEA

We are often tempted to trust ourselves instead of trusting Jesus, or to believe what sounds good to us instead of believing God's Word. We must guard against such teaching and thinking.

BIBLE CONVERSATION *15 MINUTES*

Having described what a good elder should be, Paul now tells about the need for Titus and those elders to combat false teaching. He mentions the "circumcision party" in particular. In both of the other places this phrase occurs in the New Testament (Acts 11:2 and Galatians 2:12), the context is Jewish believers who kept themselves separate from Gentile (non-Jewish) believers and urged other Jewish believers to do the same. It appears they also taught that Gentiles who believed in Christ had to convert to Judaism—be circumcised—in order to be Christ followers or to be more perfect Christ followers. The senior church leadership rejected this false teaching at the council in Jerusalem (see Acts 15), and Paul railed against it in his letter to the Galatians because it replaced faith in Christ with external works: "Did you receive the Spirit by the works of the law or by believing what you heard?

Are you so foolish? After beginning by the Spirit, are you now finishing by the flesh?" (Galatians 3:2–3). Titus himself, as a believing Gentile who did not get circumcised, had been a topic of some of those disputes (see Galatians 2:3–5).

With this background in mind, have someone read **Titus 1:10–16** aloud. Then discuss the questions below.

Given the description of Crete, what might make it difficult to follow Christ if you lived there, and how are the churches part of the problem? How is this similar to where you live today?

How might Crete also be a place of opportunity for a mission-minded or reform-minded church? Again, how is the same true for where you live today?

Verse 15 suggests the false teachers were claiming to be purer because they kept Jewish rituals. But Paul says true purity flows from right belief, not outward ritual. According to this passage, why is it so evil and dangerous to trust in your own, outward superiority instead of in Jesus?

****

Now read the following article as a group. Take turns reading it aloud, and then answer the discussion questions.

TRUTH AMID THE LIARS

5 MINUTES

Crete was a mess in all sorts of ways. Clearly, they needed help. More precisely, they needed leadership. Think about this: it is likely that some Cretans had become believers many years prior to Titus's arrival. Acts 2 says there were Cretans present when Peter preached his very first gospel message on Pentecost in Jerusalem. They undoubtedly took the good news back home with them and proclaimed Jesus Christ to their communities in Crete. More people repented and believed all over the island—just as they had in Jerusalem.

But hold on. That initial thrust was perhaps thirty years before Titus got to the island! Who knows how many Cretans had been converted in those years? Yet these believers seem to have remained disorganized, susceptible, struggling, and in need of leadership.

Additionally, Crete was not an easy place to live as a Christian. It was known for its busy ports, its prosperous urban centers (Homer called it "Crete of the hundred cities"), and its panoply of idolatrous temples from an impressive array of civilizations. There was something for everybody on Crete! Vineyards, amphitheaters, spectacular architecture, Roman baths, every evidence of "cities gone wild" could be found on Crete. Bottom line: Crete was notorious for its unbridled culture. Sound familiar?

The most talked-about vice of Cretan culture was deception. The whole Roman Empire snickered at how wickedly deceptive Cretans could be. Even their own prophets recognized how awful they were! Deception was palpable all over the island. And sadly, but not shockingly, deception had made its way into the community of Christ followers. That is evident as Paul instructs Titus about how to lead in that unique setting.

In this section, Paul reminds Titus that the truth of the gospel is, well, TRUTH! It is the divine light that shatters the darkness of sin and unbelief. Truth corrects twisted thinking. Truth turns defilement and ignorance into purity and wisdom. Truth turns the spotlight on worldly lust and exposes it for what it truly is. When Titus meets up with "rebellious people, full of empty talk and deception," he needs to expose and shatter their unbridled lies with TRUTH.

This is a page right out of Jesus's playbook. When Jesus stepped foot on planet Earth, he did so as light shining in darkness (John 1:5). Darkness ran for cover. But Jesus taught that those who recognized and received the truth would come running into the light. "Anyone who lives by the truth comes to the light, so that his works may be shown to be accomplished by God" (John 3:21).

Followers of Christ are people of the light. We don't walk in darkness any longer. And when we band together to form communities (local churches), walking in truth forms the strong bond of our unity! "If we walk in the light as he himself is in the light, we have fellowship with one another, and the blood of Jesus his Son cleanses us from all sin" (1 John 1:7).

Truth is a guiding beacon for the collective of Christ followers, the local church. Therefore, deception has no place in the church. Titus would have to confront the lies of the secular culture, but first he had to expose and correct the lies present among God's people.

Though Titus was a young man, he was uniquely qualified for equipping the church in Crete to combat empty talk and deception—especially from the highbrow "circumcision party." Why? Titus was one of the few notable Gentile leaders at this point in the history of the church. Early in his faith, Titus had to fend off those of the circumcision party who tried to compel him to first become a Jew in order to be a real Christian. Requiring circumcision was an affront to the gospel because the action indicated that Christ's work on the cross wasn't sufficient. It's not just an "added burden" but the claim that Jesus didn't accomplish our salvation and hence *we* complete it by adding our own works to it. Later, Titus was there for the important Jerusalem council that decisively freed Gentile Christians from circumcision and other Judaizing influences. Titus was wise and doctrinally strong. He was uniquely qualified to hit those issues head-on!

Finally, Paul reminded Titus that it was not going to be enough to expose and reject deception. The followers of Christ on Crete had to feed a hunger for truth. They need to be nurtured by and nourished with truth. Pure hearts long for pure truth. Conversely, those who reject pure truth will feed instead on deception and the result will be an increasingly defiled mind and conscience.

The gospel of Jesus Christ is "truth that leads to godliness." As our minds and consciences are renewed and recalibrated away from deception and toward the pure milk of truth, life transformation inevitably follows. This gospel transformation invades every sphere and every person—which is exactly what Paul will describe in our next lesson.

DISCUSSION *10 MINUTES*

Where and how might you shine the light of truth in a dark place?

In order to shine in a dark place, what truth about Jesus would you need to know firmly for yourself? How would it need to be a light for you first?

Lesson

EXERCISE

3

ADDING TO THE GOSPEL

20 MINUTES

False teaching, or even personal false *thinking*, often comes from our bad tendency to add to Jesus and the gospel. We add some other requirement on top of pure faith in Jesus, or we add something that "feels right" to pure gospel truth—and these take over. The circumcision party added Jewishness to faith in Jesus, and likely did so because it felt right to them to add this to the gospel message. We must guard against doing the same sort of thing.

For this exercise, read through the list of ways people today might feel an urge to add to Jesus or add to what the Bible teaches. Even if you wouldn't say you officially believe any of these additions, note some that may tempt you to think or live as if you believed them, or some your community tends to live by. When the group is ready, you'll share some of your observations.

ADDING TO JESUS

Authentic faith in Jesus will lead to many good things: holy living, zeal for Christ and his kingdom, and cherished teaching and traditions. But none of these should become a way we think we earn our salvation or deserve God's approval by our own merit. We are saved only through turning from sin and placing our faith in Christ alone—not in ourselves or any entitlement. The righteous record Jesus freely gives us is our right standing before God, and his transforming grace is why and how we work hard at doing good. Anything more is adding to Jesus.

❏ Jesus Plus Heritage

I feel secure before God because my family always has practiced faith, or because my culture gets things right, or because my church tradition is the most correct or most devout.

❏ Jesus Plus Getting My Life in Order

I feel like I can't really come to Jesus or ask him for any help until I first fix some problem areas in my life.

❏ Jesus Plus Good Behavior

I can't really feel secure in Jesus or approved by God until I show sufficient progress in my growth in godly living—and my progress has never really felt sufficient enough.

❏ Jesus Plus Enough Sincerity

I understand that the heart-level change of repentance and faith, not external good works, is how I come to Christ—but I wonder if my heart has been sincere enough. I need to work up more sincerity to be sure.

❏ Jesus Plus Superior Theology

My understanding of Scripture truth is on track, and my church avoids the errors most churches make, so I feel good about my status before God.

❏ Jesus Plus Emotionalism

I try to avoid "dry" faith. When I feel the Spirit moving and I get caught up in close-to-God moments, I feel good about my status before him.

❏ Jesus Plus Certain Gifts

I'm pretty sure God has given me the spiritual gift of _____. That's a good sign I've reached a higher level (or it will be, when I get that gift).

❏ Jesus Plus My Service

I've reached the point where I'm really sacrificing for Jesus, his kingdom, or his church (or I need to reach that point). My commitment makes me feel good about my standing with God.

❏ Jesus Plus My Non-Service

I stay away from superficial things like church, so my faith is purer.

❏ Jesus Plus Success

I feel okay as a believer when my family life, child raising, career, or some other marker of success looks in order.

❏ Jesus Plus _____ (Add your own.)

ADDING TO THE BIBLE

Often, when we add to Jesus it's because we first allowed ourselves to add to the Bible. Any discussion of truth in the church—from casual conversations, to sermons and faith statements—ought to spring from what God teaches us in Scripture. Anything else is adding to the Bible.

❐ The Bible Plus Tradition

I'm pretty sure the way we've always done it or said it is the biblical way, and you'd have a hard time convincing me otherwise.

❐ The Bible Plus What Sounds Right

If it fits the way I like to think and sounds like it might come from the Bible, that's good enough for me. People should get to believe and say what they think.

❐ The Bible Plus What Feels Right

If it ends up making me or others feel closer to God, it must have come from God. The Bible probably supports it, and you shouldn't tell me it doesn't.

❐ The Bible Plus Sensitivity

I want to follow the Bible, but it's important that I not offend anyone or let them think I'm backward or insensitive.

❐ The Bible Plus a Good Experience

Of course I follow the Bible, but I end up in the church or group that's the most fun or best fits my style.

❐ The Bible Plus _____ (Add your own.)

When the group is ready, share some of the items you picked. How do you get tempted to live or think as if they were true? Why do you think you do this?

Try to explain why the additions you picked are dangerous. How does the addition take emphasis or praise away from Jesus and put it on you? How does it rob you of joy, or of confidence, or of a worshipful attitude?

How can you draw closer to Jesus and have him help you stay on track?

WRAP-UP AND PRAYER *10 MINUTES*

Prayer is one of the best ways to leave behind the other things we trust and lean instead on God. Especially if this lesson brought up pride or insecurities you'd rather not admit to others, make sure you admit them to God and ask for his help. Repentance and true faith in Jesus are gifts received from him, so ask!

4

TRUTH AND GODLY LIVING

BIG IDEA

Gospel truth makes powerful teaching that has huge implications for how we live daily, whatever our role in society or the family.

BIBLE CONVERSATION *15 MINUTES*

NOTE: Today's passage includes two spots that require some explanation.

1. At the end of the passage, Paul refers to slaves (or "bond-servants" in some translations) in a way that might seem to condone slavery. But it's important to realize that although Roman-world masters sometimes could be cruel, bond-service in that world was different in several ways from the evil of slavery as practiced, for instance, in the early United States. Roman bond-service was not race-based nor dependent on man-stealing. Bondservants had rights: they could own property and work to buy their release, and many examples in the Bible show them given significant honors and responsibilities. Still, Paul suggests in Philemon that the gospel might cause masters to release

their bondservants. This means we should conclude that if abuses like those practiced in the U.S. had been prevalent in the Roman Empire, Paul would have condemned them severely as inconsistent with the gospel of Christ.

2. Verse 5 mentions young women being "workers at home." This doesn't preclude vocational work, especially since during the time when Titus was written, most work of any kind was performed at home. Being attentive to the work of the home doesn't necessarily correspond to the responsibilities associated with being a "homemaker" today. Paul's main instruction seems to be that these women put family needs ahead of personal endeavors.

Although the evils of slavery and the work of women are both important topics for believers to engage, neither is a main topic in this lesson because they are not the most central topics to this passage of Scripture. The main point here is that sound teaching will lead to godly living whatever one's place in society. Verse 11 stresses "all people." Rather than wonder about our rank and role, we should see that we *all* have the far greater honor of living in a way that adorns Christ. _How we work_ carries much more dignity than _what we do,_ and coming to grips with that truth is the real challenge this passage poses to anyone (male or female, servant or master) who reads it.

The passage begins with what could be a summary job description not just for Titus, but for any pastor: "Proclaim things consistent with sound teaching." Paul then gives specifics various members of the church might need to hear. Have someone read **Titus 2:1–11** aloud. Then discuss the questions below.

Look through Paul's instructions again. What are some general principles of a godly life that seem to apply to all the groups Paul addresses? How might they be helpful in your own church today?

If your pastor were to "proclaim sound teaching" to you based on your role in society or in your family, which of these items would he focus on, and why?

Sober-minded
dignified
Self-controlled
Sound in faith
in love + in
steadfastness

Consider how even a bondservant with menial tasks is able to adorn the gospel simply by working hard and not being argumentative (vv. 9–10). Pick one of your daily tasks, and tell how you might make Jesus look attractive by how you do it.

Home: *I could be more organized + neat at home. Since I don't enjoy organization, I can do it to please my wife + give Jesus the credit.*

Work: *I can offer to do things for others that are beyond my immediate responsibilities.*

****

Now read the article by this book's author. Take turns reading it aloud, switching readers at each paragraph, and discuss the questions when you finish.

Lesson

BEAUTIES AND BLASPHEMIES

5 MINUTES

Abraham Kuyper famously wrote, "There is not a square inch in the whole domain of our human life of which Christ, who is Sovereign of all, does not cry: Mine!"[2] The sovereign lordship of Jesus Christ is not just a theological concept; it is to be visible in our lives. Remember that this letter began by asserting that an acceptance and embrace of the truth of the gospel leads to godliness—holy living. In this section, the apostle offers Titus specific and targeted instructions for every Christ follower of every age and station of life. Every Christian must be taught how to set things right and move toward godliness.

Take note that God's church beautifully represents the full spectrum of society. Paul addresses the old, the young, the marrieds, the children. Even Titus himself gets tailormade instructions. The church is a multigenerational family, and *all* need to be taught how to express godliness in their individual spheres of life. The citizens of Crete need to see that Jesus has come to the island and he means to change everything and everyone!

---

2 Abraham Kuyper, "Sphere Sovereignty," a speech at the inauguration of the Free University of Amsterdam in 1880, trans. George Kamps, p. 26, http://www.reformationalpublishingproject.com/pdf_books/Scanned_Books_PDF/SphereSovereignty_English.pdf.

Note one more thing: Titus is to *proclaim* these things to the people. It was not enough to lead by example. People must be *told* what is right and what accords with God's truth. Don't pass over this point too quickly. What a challenging task Titus was given! Do you remember the description of Titus's audience? The Cretans (in their own words) are evil, lying, lazy gluttons. Yikes! Do you think they will take kindly to hearing the truth about their lives?

Titus is bringing good news of salvation in Jesus Christ, a message that offers the hope of eternal life to all who receive it. But that message from God is like a light that suddenly bursts onto the scene, exposing the minds, consciences, and lives of those who have been living in the darkness of unbelief.

Hearing the truth of the gospel always reveals to us places where we are making a mess of things. Even as followers of Christ, we continue to struggle with sin and unbelief. God's message of grace, like the gospel commands that Paul issues in our passage today, reveals places where our hearts resist God's mercy in favor of our own sinful desires. So, Titus has to *tell them*—all of them, all of us—how to live the new life we have in Christ. Titus was not to soft-sell the truth or adapt it to make it more palatable. Titus was to teach in a way that remained true and consistent with the truth of the gospel. It might not make him a very popular preacher!

While seeing more of our sin doesn't seem like it, it is good news (it is always good to hear the truth), even though it can be hard to take. We can find ourselves resisting the truth. We aren't always eager to be told what to do. There is a little bit of Cretan in all of us.

Because we know that tendency firsthand, we can also be reluctant to tell others what is true about them. It can be difficult to point out someone's flaws to them even when we know that telling them the truth is good and will lead to their joy. Like Titus, we have to be reminded to speak the truth and help people know what godliness looks like in their lives. The only way to do this well, is to continue to ask the Holy Spirit to reveal our own brokenness in deeper ways, so that we can come alongside of others as fellow strugglers, who need Jesus just as much as they do.

As you look carefully at what is required of each Christ follower in different spheres of life, note what is at stake. It is put to us in two ways: first in the negative and then in the positive.

From the negative perspective, if we resist or reject this call to godly living, verse 5 says we run the risk of slandering God's Word. This is strong language. The English word *blasphemy* comes from the Greek *blasphemeo* used here. When people say terrible and untruthful things about God, we call that blasphemy. And when the lives of Christ followers don't align with God's truth, people may say terrible and untruthful things about God's Word. Verse 8 says opponents of the church are looking for opportunities to say bad things about us. We mustn't give them the opportunity by rejecting the call to godliness while simultaneously saying we hold to the truth.

Stated positively, when we align our lives with the truth, we have the opportunity to "adorn the teaching of God our Savior in everything" (v. 10). The word *adorn* is the Greek *kosmeo*, where we get our English word *cosmetics*—to make beautiful. The most powerful thing we can do as we proclaim the truth of the gospel is to make it beautiful to the hearer as they see us living out the truth in every sphere of life.

Okay, dive further into our passage in Titus through the discussion questions and exercise. Ask God to show you how to be bold in proclaiming the gospel and also bold in applying the gospel in your own life. (Be careful, this might hurt—but it is GOOD!)

DISCUSSION *10 MINUTES*

What are you willing to say to fellow believers when necessary and where do you hold back? How much of your speaking up (or holding back) is care for them, and how much is self-interest?

Self interest is certainly part of some relationships.

When you think about your behavior in the world, how often do you consider that you are either blaspheming or beautifying Jesus in all you do? Give an example of the difference this realization makes.

We are ambassadors of Christ. The reality is that people judge christianity by our behavior. + sincerity.

Lesson

WHEN JESUS IS ENOUGH

20 MINUTES

Remember that the false teachers at the end of chapter 1 did not consider what Jesus did for them to be enough. They felt a need to add external regulations they could do. Their mind-set was, "I need to do/get more to be okay." But a gospel mind-set is different. It says, "I have all I need in Jesus, so I already am okay." This gospel truth frees us to lovingly serve God and others.

For this exercise, we'll look at some of the items in Paul's list of virtues that are "consistent with sound teaching." Each comes with a description of what happens when you fail to believe that Jesus is enough for you, and also what happens when you believe the gospel that Jesus is enough. On your own, read the descriptions and note some that fit you or ways you hope to grow. When the group is ready, you'll have a chance to share some of your findings.

RESPECT FOR OTHERS

When I don't believe Jesus is enough: It bothers me if others get praise when I don't, or if I'm not shown due respect by my kids, spouse, parents, boss, coworkers, friends, or people at church. I get angry, or I withdraw, or I subtly show off to try to earn more respect.

46

When Jesus is enough: I know I have the honor of being God's child, so I don't need to chase more respect for myself. I can concentrate instead on taking the low place and showing respect to others. I'm even willing to look foolish if it helps others learn about Jesus.

SELF-CONTROL

When I don't believe Jesus is enough: I am easily bothered if I don't get my way or miss out on something I was hoping for. When I sense that happening, I lose control and might lie, cheat, be unkind to others, or "beat myself up."

When Jesus is enough: My hope is in the lasting blessings I have in Christ, not in worldly success. I know my Father will give me everything I need, so I can stay in control even when life seems to go badly.

LOVE

When I don't believe Jesus is enough: I need love. I count on my spouse, children, parents or some other relationship to give me enough love—as perfectly as possible. When they fail, I may get demanding or depressed, or search elsewhere.

When Jesus is enough: I know I am loved eternally and thoroughly by my Father in heaven and the Savior who died for me. Instead of having to go looking for love, I can spend my life looking for ways to give love.

AVOIDING SLANDER

When I don't believe Jesus is enough: Gossip, and putting other people down, helps me feel better about myself. I tend to talk about the sins of others more often than I confess my own sins.

When Jesus is enough: I know I am a big sinner who's been forgiven and that I am still God's work-in-progress, so I'm willing to admit my sin and accept correction. It's okay for others to know how desperately I need Jesus.

INTEGRITY

When I don't believe Jesus is enough: I'm a different person when people are watching than I am when I'm alone. My pious words don't match what I'm thinking, and my pious actions don't match what I do in secret. For example, I might pray in a group but seldom pray by myself.

When Jesus is enough: God's Word to me is my soul's sure anchor. I really believe he is the Savior who died for me, the Father who loves me forever, the Helper who comforts and guides me, and the One I will glorify and enjoy forever. I live with the sense that he is always beside me.

FAITHFULNESS

When I don't believe Jesus is enough: I claim to be loyal to my friends, employer, family, and church, but I'm really loyal to myself. I mostly use my relationships to get ahead or make myself look good, not to faithfully serve others.

When Jesus is enough: I know Jesus is faithful to serve me. He helps me die to myself in this world, and he is trustworthy to give me honor and a great inheritance in the next world. Because he is my faithful Savior, I can be a faithful servant who gives up my own comforts and dignity to advance his kingdom and tell the gospel.

HUMILITY IN SPEECH

When I don't believe Jesus is enough: My comments are often calculated to build myself up or draw attention to my achievements—because I need for people to notice. If anyone points out a weakness in me, I am inclined to talk back, make excuses, shift blame, or mention how others are even worse than me.

When Jesus is enough: Because Jesus is my strength, my talk about myself is mostly about weaknesses. I already enjoy my Father's perfect approval. Now I want people to notice Jesus more than I want them to notice me.

When the group is ready, share some of your thoughts. Which items are personally revealing, and why? How do you hope to grow in the gospel?

The point of this exercise is not for you to feel discouraged about the amount of growth ahead of you, but to see how believing the gospel can help. What, specifically, do you want to believe about Jesus's love for you, and how might that help you?

Faith (belief in the gospel) is not generated by self-effort out of your strength. Rather, it is *received* from God in your weakness. How can you work on these things in a way that seeks God, looking to him to give you confidence that the gospel is true?

WRAP-UP AND PRAYER *10 MINUTES*

Prayer is a key part of seeking God. Ask him to help you believe the gospel. When you pray this, you acknowledge that your self-effort can't change your heart. Your Father wants you to turn to him and rely on him to change you, so he loves to hear you pray out of your weakness and need.

5

TRUTH AND GOD'S GRACE

BIG IDEA

The grace of God is our teacher. A constant awareness of the many gifts that are ours in Christ will train us to move out in mission, eager to do good works.

BIBLE CONVERSATION *15 MINUTES*

Having described the good works of a believer's life, Paul now gives the reason and motivation for those good works: "For the grace of God has appeared," and that grace teaches us how to live. Have someone read **Titus 2:11–15** aloud, then discuss the questions below:

Paul says the grace of God is not just a doctrine, but our teacher (or "trainer" in some English translations). Look at the gifts God graciously gives us in verses 13 and 14. How might these teach you the best way to live?

Specifically, how might these gracious gifts of God make you eager about the work of "salvation for all people"—a life of mission?

Why might Paul be so adamant, in verse 15, that Titus preach with such insistence about these gracious gifts from God? What makes them so important?

Which of these gracious gifts from God do you sometimes disregard, or seldom think about, and why? How might that be harmful to you?

✶✶✶✶

Read the following article aloud, taking turns by paragraph. Then discuss the questions at the end of the article.

Lesson

5

LOOKING BACK AND LOOKING AHEAD

5 MINUTES

These five verses are packed. It is like taking the whole glorious message of the gospel and condensing it into one paragraph. New Testament scholar Gordon Fee speaks of the rich "theological grist" contained in these few words.[3] You could dig into these few words for a very long time and not exhaust the depth of meaning contained here.

God's grace burst into our dark world in Jesus Christ. The incarnation, the crucifixion, and the resurrection of Jesus Christ brought good news of salvation to all people. We don't have to remain bound in our sin and blinded by the darkness of our unbelief. Jesus has come for us! We can be rescued!

Slow down and ponder the opening phrase of this passage: "The grace of God has appeared, bringing salvation for all people." What is Paul teaching Titus? He is reminding Titus and the Cretan believers that the gospel that saved them is still at work and will keep spreading to the ends of the earth. It isn't just the unbelievers on Crete who can find hope and eternal life. This message of good

---

3 Gordon Fee, *1 & 2 Timothy, Titus*, New International Bible Commentary (Peabody, MA: Hendrickson, 1988), 193.

news remains powerful and effective for all who hear it, including those of us who are already believers. We are to proclaim it and live it in order to bring more and more people to the truth that will lead to godliness.

But there is more. It is right for us to look back to see what Jesus Christ already accomplished in bringing salvation to the world. But we must also look forward to what he is about to do! Here, the apostle uniquely adds a motivation—perhaps better, an *aspiration*—to move Titus (and Cretans, and us!) toward the truth that leads to godliness. When we *aspire* toward something, we have a strong, "soulish" passion to strain toward a goal. Paul is pointing us to a gospel-fueled aspiration: the glorious return of Jesus Christ.

Notice the order here—it is important. Paul first compels Titus to look back to what Jesus Christ has done for us (v. 11). Recalling what Jesus accomplished for us in his rescue operation motivates us to shake off our old way of life and to live in a sensible, righteous, and godly way in this present age (v. 12). Paul reminds us that the gospel doesn't free us from obedience, but frees us to obey God as we say "no" to things that don't honor him. Thank you, Jesus, for coming and giving me a new life!

But then Paul goes further. Looking back is essential and effective. It absolutely impacts our lives in the present. But this present age is only temporary. There is far more to come. By placing our trust in the finished work of Christ (accomplished in the past) we have been given a new destiny—a blessed hope for the future (v. 13). This is not the kind of "hope" that is uncertain, like some kind of wishful feeling. No, Christ followers are given a confident, certain expectation of Christ's return for them.

Let's be honest. The second coming of Christ often seems fantastical to us, maybe even too extraordinary to be true. But don't forget—there were many, many people who doubted Jesus Christ would come the first time in his incarnation. How could such a thing be? Would God really become a man and die for sinners? What kind of myth is that? But he did! Every promise came true. And just as Jesus came to bring salvation for all people, so he is going to come again. It is *that* certain.

The Bible teaches that this present age is temporary. It will terminate. It has a shelf life. The days on this earth in which God's call for salvation goes out to all people will come to a close. There is a coming day when Jesus will return. This time he will not *bring* salvation, but *complete* it. The coming day will be the final curtain call. Jesus will rescue his followers, will rightfully judge all who have rejected him, and return the created world to the way it was intended to be since the beginning of time.

Until that day, we wait with expectation. What does looking forward to the blessed hope do for Christ followers? It gives even more fuel to live for him right now! Jesus humbled himself by leaving heaven in order to serve us. He then went through the humiliation of the cross to save us. He rose again in order to defeat sin and the grave for us. He will come again to lead us to a place prepared for his family (that's us!), where sin and death will never be seen again.

Friends, Jesus has done *and will do* everything for us. Doesn't that motivate you to live for him while we wait for him to come and get us? Cretans should gladly put away their lying, evil, gluttonous ways to love and serve the one who has done it all for them. And so should we.

Let us drink deeply of the rich truths packed into these few verses. And then let us tell others—with hope and with sobering truth. No time for cowardice. No time for hesitancy. Let's tell the world about this incredible grace!

DISCUSSION *10 MINUTES*

How much is the second coming of Jesus a motivation in your life? How might you live differently if the second coming were the event you most looked forward to, constantly on your mind?

The article says this is no time for cowardice or hesitancy. What causes fear or hesitation when you consider ways to show mercy to others or tell them about Jesus?

What part of today's passage in Titus best addresses your fears and hesitations?

EXERCISE

THE GOSPEL AND GOOD WORKS

20 MINUTES

Both looking back to what Jesus has already done for us and looking ahead to what he promises ought to make us "eager to do good works" (v. 14). For this exercise, you'll practice looking both directions, using descriptions of the gospel and Bible verses. Work through the exercise on your own first, then discuss it when the group is ready.

Paul's announcement that "the grace of God has appeared, bringing salvation for all people" ought to give you a mission-minded excitement. So start by having a specific "mission" in mind for this exercise. Think of a way the gospel hope you have might compel you to go out, loving and serving others. (Don't worry, no one is asking you to commit, only to have a concrete "what if . . ." in mind.) Your example might be:

❏ A way you could reach new people by proclaiming the gospel, anything from becoming a church-planting missionary to starting a conversation about Jesus with your neighbor

❏ A way you might work to bring healing and restoration to some part of our sin-broken world, far away or near, as a sign of Jesus's kingdom

❏ A sacrificial way to be part of sending others

❏ A way to better love and lay down your life for the people already around you—family, coworkers, friends, those in church—in how you lead, serve, or speak to them

My "mission" might be to _lead people to Jesus through my involvement in their lives & then give credit to Jesus_.

To go out and love others requires a constant interplay with the gospel. The gospel compels us to love others in the first place. But because loving others is hard, our mission also will drive us back to the gospel again and again, making us more grounded in Jesus's love and renewing our eagerness to keep loving others. With your example in mind, read through some ways the gospel blessings Paul mentions interact with a life on mission. Note some that encourage or challenge you.

The LOOKING-BACK gospel says I have been . . .

Loved. "He gave himself for us . . ."

❏ Having received love from Jesus, I realize there is nothing better than a life of love—giving, sacrificing, laying down my life to serve others and reach them with the gospel. "He died for all so that those who live should no longer live for themselves" (2 Corinthians 5:15).

challenge

❑ When I am rejected or mistreated, Jesus's love for me sustains me. He received the same treatment, for my sake. I know I am still loved, whatever happens.

Rescued from evil. ". . . to redeem us from all lawlessness . . ."

❑ My rescue from sin is the defining event in my life. It makes me want my whole life to be about putting sin behind me and building Christ's kingdom in its place. "He has rescued us from the domain of darkness and transferred us into the kingdom of the Son he loves" (Colossians 1:13).

challenge

❑ When evil seems to win, either because I have sinned or because my kingdom work is frustrating, I remember that I have a Savior. The evil does not own me, Jesus does.

Forgiven and counted righteous in Christ. ". . . and to cleanse for himself . . ."

❑ I don't get self-important because my good record comes from Jesus, and I don't despair because my sin is forgiven. This frees me to go out and actually love people rather than worrying about slights, my performance, or possible failure. "Just as the Lord has forgiven you, so you are also to forgive" (Colossians 3:13).

❑ When I sin while serving others, I run back to the cross to enjoy forgiveness anew. That way I keep being kind to others instead of making excuses, shifting blame to them, or pretending I've done nothing wrong.

Brought into God's family. ". . . a people for his own possession."

❑ I have a home with my Father who loves me and is always with me. I can leave all other homes and comforts behind if necessary, and go out to serve him and others. "Don't be afraid, little flock, because your Father delights to give you the kingdom. Sell your possessions and give to the poor" (Luke 12:32–33).

Challenging

❒ When it gets costly to love others and I'm tempted to give up because of what I've lost, I learn even more to enjoy being with my Father who is always there.

The LOOKING-AHEAD gospel says I can look forward to . . .

A life of joy. "We wait for the blessed hope . . ."

❒ The rewards of the life to come cause me to store up treasures in heaven by living for God's glory and the needs of others. The path of humility Jesus took is also the path to lasting joy. "Whatever you do, do it from the heart, as something done for the Lord and not for people, knowing that you will receive the reward of an inheritance from the Lord" (Colossians 3:23–24).

❒ When the pleasures of this life are taken from me and rewards are few, I press on with the next life's rewards and pleasures in mind. — *wrong motive!*

Judgment and vindication. ". . . the appearing of our great God and Savior . . ."

❒ The Judge who will come for me is also the Savior who has already taken my punishment, so I wait for him confidently and want the same assurance for others. "Our citizenship is in heaven, and we eagerly wait for a Savior from there" (Philippians 3:20).

❒ When I am mocked for what I believe or told that future generations will say I am wrong, I remember that Jesus's return is my true future and he will prove me right.

A renewed world with God. ". . . the glory of Jesus Christ."

❐ Jesus is reclaiming this world. It is my high privilege to join in the first stage of his kingdom's arrival, happening now, by doing good in the world in anticipation of his return to reign. "As you go, proclaim: 'The kingdom of heaven has come near.' Heal the sick, raise the dead, cleanse those with leprosy, drive out demons. Freely you received, freely give" (Matthew 10:7–8).

❐ When death or hardship or evil seems to win, I remember that I am on the side of King Jesus's new creation that is breaking in, and I keep going.

When the group is ready, share some of your results. Which descriptions or Bible verses are especially encouraging to you, and why? Which seem challenging? Which do you already consider to be big motivations in your life, and which have you seldom thought about before?

WRAP-UP AND PRAYER *10 MINUTES*

In addition to looking-back and looking-ahead parts of the gospel, we also have the good news of what Jesus is doing for us right now. We can be confident that he guides us and causes us to grow in the gospel. Pray together that he would do this in the ways you've discussed in this lesson.

Lesson

6

TRUTH AND DEVOTION

BIG IDEA

The gospel produces in us an attractive life of obedience, submission, and devotion to good works.

BIBLE CONVERSATION *15 MINUTES*

As we move into chapter 3 of Paul's letter to Titus, the apostle is still showing how gospel truths lead to godly living. Chapter 2 began with how-to-live instructions and then gave the gospel reasons behind that kind of life. The first part of chapter 3 repeats the same pattern. Have someone read **Titus 3:1–8** aloud. Then discuss the questions below.

What would people in your community think if Christ followers today consistently lived according to verses 1 and 2? Which item listed there sounds most striking to you, and why?

Verses 4–7 begin with a second announcement (the first was in 2:11) that salvation for all people has appeared in our age. Look through the gospel truths mentioned. What would it be like to live in a place where none of those truths have been proclaimed, and what would it mean to hear them for the first time?

Why must those gospel truths be something Titus teaches again and again, even to Christ followers who have already heard and believed them many times?

****

Continue by reading the article aloud, switching readers at each paragraph break. When you finish, discuss the questions that follow.

Lesson

6

ARTICLE

THE BEAUTY OF SUBMISSION

5 MINUTES

Submit! Obey! Hey, Paul, this is not exactly the way to win over a crowd. I'm not sure how the Cretans would have responded to this, but I know that people in Iowa, where I live, won't be too jazzed.

This Bible passage is an incredibly important section. Paul did not suddenly become a moralist or a legalist. The opening instructions (albeit bold and assertive) are anchored in the gospel. More than that, the purpose of following these directives is *not* to win the favor of God or others with impeccable behavior. That's way too simplistic and shallow. Submission and obedience to authority spring from the gospel—they are the fruit of a life transformed by Christ. What's more, submission and obedience are powerful tools in drawing outsiders to the gospel.

Wait, let's start with that last point. How does our submission and obedience to authority draw others to the gospel of Christ? Let's be candid: slandering, fighting, being unkind, and resisting people with authority over us—these things came as naturally and easy to Cretans as they do to every other people group on the planet. Nobody has to teach a toddler these traits. They show up in the highest echelons of Wall Street (often well-manicured, but ruthless nonetheless) as well as in the slums of Calcutta. It is a universal distinguishing mark of humanity. We are a race of rebels.

And so, when you encounter someone who is kind and gentle to all people, they stand out! You are drawn to them. When someone who is kind and gentle because of Christ is stopped on the street and asked, "Man, what makes you tick? How'd you get so nice?" they can quickly point to the gospel. "Oh, I used to be such a fool. I bucked authority, I was deceived and I did my share of deceiving. Frankly, I was a mess. But then I discovered the kindest person who ever walked this earth . . ." Imagine how that example must have stood out in first-century Crete, given their reputation for terrible behavior. That type of example still stands out today, when so many are still so far from God, and Christians are often perceived to be unkind and hypocritical.

One of the most visible expressions of godlessness is not the way we treat God, but the terrible way we treat our fellow human beings. Malice, envy, and hatefulness are as blatantly and embarrassingly visible on the school playground as they are in the highest offices of our national government. People really do detest one another. To make that point stick, Paul uses two different words for hate almost on top of one another in verse 3. "We are full of odious hatefulness which causes us to throw detestable hatred toward each other" (that's my expanded translation).

But as transformed followers of Christ, we should no longer talk down to people. We aren't supposed to be smug and patronizing. We know very well where the path of reckless thinking and behavior leads. We are embarrassed by our past hateful ways and convicted by the places where we still blow it today. But mostly, we are humbled by the fact that God has given, and continues to give us, a fresh start. It is our joy to show others the path of freedom, kindness, and salvation. The gospel not only transforms us, it moves us to reach out to others even when they don't look, talk, think or act like we do.

Look at the contrast Paul gives in verse 4. Right after the dark description of humanity: BAM! God bursts onto the scene with his kindness and love. There it is. This is where we find our source of supernatural kindness to blow the darkness of rebellion and hatred away. It is the good news of salvation in God our Savior. Malice, envy, and even hatred don't stand a chance against the magnificent love of God.

This causes Paul to write another tightly compressed explanation of the gospel in verses 5–7. (The ink is still drying from the former one at the end of chapter 2.) He can't help it. He has to restate it again—and it never gets old.

Don't minimize the way these truths have come near to us. When does God's loving kindness show up? God appears to us even as he sees the fullest, deepest, ugliest parts of us. There we were wallowing in foolishness, enslaving ourselves to toxic passions, and fomenting hate. God didn't wait for us to get our act together and clean ourselves up. When we were at our worst, his love came to us.

Are you ready for what this means? It means that neither are we to wait for others to earn our love and kindness. We love because we have been loved. We forgive because we have been forgiven. We are kind because we have been shown inexpressible kindness. As Christ followers, we have been born again into a new life. Even though we sinned a lot (don't minimize it—a LOT!), the Spirit is poured on us *abundantly*. "Where sin multiplied, grace multiplied even more" (Romans 5:20).

This is a beautiful expression of the gospel, and it puts the love of Christ on full display. Cretans need to see this kindness and so does our world. Unbelievers should marvel at the transformation that is so markedly distinct it could only be supernatural. Suddenly, submission and obedience look pretty attractive after all.

DISCUSSION *10 MINUTES*

How do you react to the idea that submission and obedience are attractive and desirable?

If you can, describe a time in your life when you practiced submission or humility and were able to see the beauty in it. What made it attractive, or how did God use it to build his kingdom?

How does the submission and humility of Jesus during his life on earth encourage you when you are challenged to live the same way?

Lesson

EXERCISE

A GOSPEL STATEMENT

20 MINUTES

Verses 4–7 in our passage sound like a creed or summary gospel statement, perhaps some words the church on Crete could memorize and use as the basis for their belief and vision. For this exercise, you will go through each part of that statement and apply it to your life and your interests, enriching this creed with personal details meaningful to you.

Work through the exercise on your own first, completing sentences where there are blanks. Write your responses or take notes if that helps you remember. Try to respond in ways specific to you. When the group is ready, you'll have a chance to share some of your responses.

"But when the kindness of God our Savior and his love for mankind appeared . . ."

I am especially thrilled that the good news of God's love has appeared to people who _____

_____

_____

_____.

". . . he saved us—not by works of righteousness that we had done, but according to his mercy . . ."

God has been especially merciful in bringing the gospel to me, since I am so undeserving and _____

_____

_____

_____.

". . . through the washing of regeneration and renewal by the Holy Spirit. He poured out his Spirit on us abundantly through Jesus Christ our Savior . . ."

Thanks to God's work in me, I have experienced spiritual renewal in my life. People can see this by how I _____

_____

_____

_____.

". . . so that, having been justified by grace, we may become heirs with the hope of eternal life."

I praise God that I am already counted righteous in Christ, and I am eager for the day when my salvation is completed and I ___

_____

_____

_____.

When the group is ready, share some of your responses. If you were to pick one of these truths to become a personal statement summarizing your delight in Jesus, which would it be, and why?

Where and when might you tell others your personal statement, either to introduce the gospel to them or to encourage someone who already believes?

How else are these truths "good and profitable" for you, encouraging you to devote yourself to good works, as Paul says in verse 8?

WRAP-UP AND PRAYER *10 MINUTES*

As part of your prayer time together, include thanks to God for his salvation and his work in you.

7

TRUTH AND HUMILITY

BIG IDEA

Gospel teaching should produce a climate of rigorous obedience to God that is adorned with humility, not stained by an attitude of superiority.

BIBLE CONVERSATION *15 MINUTES*

In our previous passage, Paul presented a gospel statement he called trustworthy and profitable. In today's passage, he contrasts that statement with discussions he labels unprofitable and worthless. Have someone read **Titus 3:8–15** aloud (it starts with the verse that calls the gospel statement from last time "trustworthy"). Then discuss the questions below:

How is the character of those people devoted to the gospel statement different from the character of those devoted to foolish debates? Think of several differences you can infer from the passage.

Some theological debates are necessary or help us discover deep things about God. But what guidelines for theological discussion might be wise, based on this passage? Think of several.

One worthwhile good work Paul has in mind is support for traveling missionaries. What principles for missionary support does this passage give us? How might you implement them?

∗ ∗ ∗ ∗

Now read the article aloud, taking turns by paragraph, and then discuss the questions that follow it.

WHEN PEOPLE LOVE TO ARGUE

5 MINUTES

As we said from the beginning, Crete was a hot mess. But now the glorious gospel has come to the island. Now the transformation has begun. Titus has arrived to set things right. By God's grace, the rebels who were full of empty talk and deception are encountering the truth that leads to godliness. God's boundless love and kindness is turning Crete upside down (make that "right side up").

Titus has his work cut out for him. Just like today, he's not the only one seeking to influence the church. We've seen that false teachers have gotten there before him. They are in it for personal gain, and their influence is bringing confusion and ruin to entire households. Titus has to proclaim God's good news, but he also has to confront the wicked false teachers. That's no easy task! This is why Paul circles back to a sobering reminder about false teaching before he puts down the quill and hands this scroll to the courier headed for Crete.

It would be easy for Titus to get bogged down in endless squabbles and verbal spars with the false teachers. They only seek to disrupt, discourage, and confuse. If they can get Titus entangled in their snare of debates, they will muzzle him from getting the good news out to the rest of the island. Paul needs Titus to steer clear of that demonic tactic.

We can't be certain what precisely these false teachers brought in their bag of tricks. The content of the debates, speculative genealogies, quarrels, and disputes have been lost to history. And that is likely by God's design. Those who want to quarrel will change topics and tactics often in order to keep the argument going. They aren't looking for answers or resolution. They are looking for a fight. Titus must see that and walk away. There is nothing to be gained in that battle.

Sometimes those disputes come right into the church. A seemingly well-intentioned man or woman raises a divisive issue, and then another, and then another. Pretty soon a pattern emerges, and we have to say something. *Wait, are you here to join us in a pursuit of truth that leads to godliness? Or are you here to harass us with divisive opinions that seem to have no end (other than to draw attention away from the truth that leads to godliness)?*

This is a tough lesson for most of us. Titus is clearly instructed to warn them directly. Perhaps this person is truly confused or sincerely concerned about a matter. If so, that will become obvious. Remember, Christ followers are no longer quarrelsome; that is the old Cretan way. True Christ followers are kind, gentle, and teachable.

Paul's instructions about responding to these contentious debates is telling. The message of the gospel is to be front and center. The gospel "saying" of verses 4–7 is trustworthy, not the debates about minor issues or controversial topics. Therefore, Titus is to insist on the message of God's salvation being heard over and over, clearly and powerfully. Why? So that those who have believed in God, and his Good News of grace and salvation, will be devoted to doing good works which demonstrate God's power and not get sidelined with internal debates and quarrels. This is why Paul is issuing such stern instructions in verses 9–11 about rejecting those who insist on creating controversy. He knows that unless the gospel stays front and center, the believers in Crete will become distracted and fall into quarrelsome divisions. They will stop modeling the type of winsome transformation Paul has just outlined in verses 1–3. Their witness to their unbelieving neighbors will be lost and the spread of the gospel on Crete will be halted. Instead, Titus must focus on what is central—the message of God's love and grace toward broken sinners, who desperately need to be saved. That gospel focus is to characterize our lives and our churches as well, so that it has its intended effect—a wholehearted devotion to doing good in our world to help others be introduced to Jesus.

Before Paul dries the ink and rolls up the parchment, he offers some endearing words to his friend and young protégé. Like a father longing to see his son, Paul asked Titus to come visit him. Nicopolis was not down the block. It would take Titus getting on a boat and sailing north to the western coastline of Greece. He also asked Titus to help others who were giving their lives for the advance of the gospel. Note the selflessness and camaraderie of these faithful workers!

The final farewell finds Paul repeating the recurring theme of this small letter: "Let our people learn to devote themselves to good works for pressing needs, so that they will not be unfruitful" (v. 14). One of the most visible expressions of truth that leads to godliness is the gospel-fueled impulse to count others as more important than yourself (see Philippians 2:3). That is the way of Jesus. Good works are not those done in solitary isolation. Gospel-fueled good works benefit others.

Dear reader, as Paul concluded this powerful and inspired letter to Titus, so receive the benediction he offers: The Lord be with your spirit. Grace be with you all.

DISCUSSION *10 MINUTES*

What makes it hard for church leaders in your culture to confront argumentative people or those who won't be corrected? Would your church leaders say you make their job easier or harder, and why?

What makes us enjoy being argumentative? What is it about the gospel that ought to change this, and how has it changed you?

A HUMBLE LIFE
20 MINUTES

The article mentioned how gospel-fueled good works are largely a matter of treating others as more important than ourselves. In Philippians, Paul explains that this others-first lifestyle follows the model of Jesus, who came down from heaven to serve, suffer, and die. When we've experienced his love, we also enter into it by having the same self-giving purpose: "Do nothing out of selfish ambition or conceit, but in humility consider others as more important than yourselves" (Philippians 2:3).

On your own, read through the descriptions of how humility is both WHAT we do and HOW we do it. Note how God is teaching you this new lifestyle. When the group is ready, you'll discuss your results. NOTE: Though it brings joy, this lifestyle is called "dying to self" for good reason: it's difficult and can feel like death. We are all still in the process of learning it, so don't be dismayed by how far you have to go; focus on where God has brought you so far.

PART 1: HUMILITY IS WHAT WE DO

At Work

I am truly happy when my coworkers receive recognition and advancement. I try to contribute to their success, value their ideas, and treat their work as more important than mine. Rather than being insecure about my job performance, I work to make their jobs easier and let them take the credit.

❑ God has made me aware that I'm naturally selfish and need to work on this.

❑ God has helped me see that this kind of life has Christ-like beauty.

❑ God has led me to begin joyfully working to live this way by

_____

_____

_____.

❑ God has given me progress in living this way by _____

_____

_____

_____.

At Home

My needs and preferences come last. I am there to serve others in my home, not to demand or assume that they serve or satisfy me. When I am called upon to lead at home, I do so with love that truly gives up my own interests. When I am called to follow at home, I do so with a good spirit.

❑ God has made me aware that I'm naturally selfish and need to work on this.

❑ God has helped me see that this kind of life has Christ-like beauty.

❏ God has led me to begin joyfully working to live this way by
_____
_____
_____.

❏ God has given me progress in living this way by _____
_____
_____
_____.

At Church

My contributions don't have to be acknowledged, and my ideas about how things should be done don't have to be accepted. I'm most happy when others' needs are met. I arrive at a service not to judge it, but as the sinner most unworthy to be there, humbled that I may come and worship the Worthy One.

❏ God has made me aware that I'm naturally selfish and need to work on this.

❏ God has helped me see that this kind of life has Christ-like beauty.

❏ God has led me to begin joyfully working to live this way by
_____
_____
_____.

❏ God has given me progress in living this way by _____
_____
_____
_____.

With Friends

In casual conversation, I feel no need to show off what I know, one-up others' stories, or have people agree with me. In deep conversation, I listen to others, admit my sins, and allow people to correct me. My friends would say I am both approachable and teachable.

❐ God has made me aware that I'm naturally selfish and need to work on this.

❐ God has helped me see that this kind of life has Christ-like beauty.

❐ God has led me to begin joyfully working to live this way by

_____

_____ .

❐ God has given me progress in living this way by _____

_____

_____ .

PART 2: HUMILITY IS ALSO HOW WE DO IT

But *how* do we achieve such humility? Paul calls this being fruitful (v. 14 in today's passage), and Jesus taught us how to be fruitful: "The one who remains in me and I in him produces much fruit, because you can do nothing without me" (John 15:5). Here we see again that we must think less of ourselves. It is humbling to realize we must stay connected to Jesus like a child holding a parent's hand. The close-to-Christ habits of Scripture reading, prayer, and churchgoing are marks of a humble believer who knows how vital it is to receive weekly, daily, and hourly grace from the True Vine.

The Bible

I read the Bible often, not for affirmation of what I'm thinking or to look impressive, but because I need to hear from my Savior. I need for him to teach me much that I don't yet know, and I need for him to encourage me with many truths I haven't yet noticed. Then I can put others first.

❒ God has made me aware that I'm naturally self-trusting and need to work on this.

❒ God has helped me see the joy of this kind of trusting life with Jesus.

❒ God has led me to begin coming near to Jesus this way by
_____
_____.

Prayer

I pray often and stay constantly aware that God is with me. My Father is both a joy to be with and my good guide and provider. When I have a hard time putting others first, my first impulse is to turn to my Father for help. He gives strength and assures me that he meets all my needs, leaving me free to live for the needs of others.

❒ God has made me aware that I'm naturally self-trusting and need to work on this.

❒ God has helped me see the joy of this kind of trusting life with Jesus.

❒ God has led me to begin coming near to Jesus this way by
_____
_____.

The Church's Worship

I consider it a supreme honor that already in this life I may worship Jesus in the midst of his people and eat at his table as we will in heaven. Also, I depend on having God's Word preached to me by his minister and sung to me by Jesus's gathered people. Without them, I feel I would be unable to put others first—so I am grateful for them all.

☐ God has made me aware that I'm naturally self-trusting and need to work on this.

☐ God has helped me see the joy of this kind of trusting life with Jesus.

☐ God has led me to begin coming near to Jesus this way by

_____

_____.

The Gospel

My prayer, Bible reading, and churchgoing are not chiefly duties I perform, but ways I am encouraged by God's grace. They remind me that I am a sinner who is forgiven, a child who is given a home, a weakling who is strengthened, and a dying person who will live forever. I go to the gospel to stay humble and grateful, which makes me willing to put others first.

☐ God has made me aware that I'm naturally self-trusting and need to work on this.

☐ God has helped me see the joy of this kind of trusting life with Jesus.

❏ God has led me to begin coming near to Jesus this way by

_____

_____.

When the group is ready, share some of your results. How has God been teaching you? How do you hope to grow more?

As this study ends, how will you keep pursuing the "knowledge of the truth that leads to godliness"? In other words, how will you stay grounded in the gospel so you can live a life of love?

WRAP-UP AND PRAYER *10 MINUTES*

Practice humble dependence on your Father by praying together for yourself and for others. You might also pray, as a group, that God would strengthen your private prayer lives. Personal prayer that secretly asks God for help is one of the chief signs of Christian humility, since no one else is around to think well of you for praying and no one else will know to give you credit for any results. So have the group pray that you would learn to be a person who prays in private.

LEADER'S NOTES

These notes provide some thoughts that relate to the study's discussion questions, especially the Bible conversation sections. The discussion leader should read these notes before the study begins. Sometimes, the leader may want to refer the group to a point found here.

However, it is important that you NOT treat these notes as a way to look up the "right answer." In most cases, the best answers will be those the group discovers *on its own* through reading and thinking about the Bible passages. You will lose the value of looking closely at what the Bible says, and taking time to think about it, if you are too quick to turn to these notes.

LESSON 1: TRUTH THAT LEADS TO GODLINESS

Paul lists several purposes behind his calling and ministry: It is for the faith of the believers God has elected. It is to give them knowledge of the truth. It is to lead them, by that knowledge, into godliness. It is to give them the sure hope of eternal life which God promised before time began. It is to be faithful to God's command in a time of wondrous revelation.

We ought to share Paul's hope and vision as we approach the book of Titus. We can prayerfully expect God's Word to build our own faith, give us knowledge of the truth, and lead us into greater godliness. We can expect it to increase our joy and hope in the life God promises, and to deepen our zeal to proclaim the good news of Jesus throughout the world in our own time.

In whatever way we might be engaged in God's great mission of advancing his kingdom, it is encouraging to see what his truth and his Word can do—how they lead to godliness and eternal life. This gives us courage to proclaim it and live it out everywhere. In addition, we ourselves constantly need to grow in faith, godliness, and hope in order to keep on taking these things to others. Happily, we have the gospel truth to give us that strength.

This truth is no mere human word, but rather God's Word to us. It deserves our utmost attentiveness—perhaps even some fear that we dare not ignore it. It deserves to be heard with great expectation, since God's Word is accompanied by his enabling power and surely will accomplish what he intends (Isaiah 55:11). It deserves to be received with joy, for it is the hope promised before time began. It deserves to be treated as life itself, for Jesus has promised, "The words that I have spoken to you are spirit and are life" (John 6:63).

LESSON 2: TRUTH AND LEADERSHIP

God's people on Crete are facing dangers both within and outside of the church. Within the church, false teaching threatens to ruin entire households. Some of these false teachers are greedy for money and willing to lie. Outside of the church, it appears that lies, laziness, drunkenness, and wild living are all familiar sins on Crete, while family difficulties, struggles with temper, and substance abuse are well-known problems people face.

It would be foolish to think God's people can overcome these concerns on their own, without support, or to think our world today is much different. Godly elders who have not succumbed to these things can show us a better way and keep the church's teaching on track. Jesus is the ultimate elder we all need, but his method is to give us local elders who live alongside us and face the same daily challenges we do. To reject their leadership is to reject his leadership.

An elder's task is a challenging one: to demonstrate to the church a life like Jesus. In the realm of teaching, this means an elder must have both compassion and courage, both gentleness for those young in the faith and firmness toward any who would lead them astray. It's hard to imagine this could be accomplished well without being a student of the Scriptures and a person of prayer, as Jesus clearly was (see Luke 2:46–47 and 5:15–16, for example).

NOTE: Verse 6 is sometimes used to assert that an elder's children must all be believers, but this interpretation is unsure because the Greek word *pistos* can also refer to faithfulness in a more general sense. It is probably best that groups not try to debate the usage here, but note the larger point that an elder must have good control of his own household if he is to lead God's household (see the parallel point in 1 Timothy 3:4–5). Also, try not to let the group get stuck on the difference between an elder (the Greek *presbuteros* in verse 5) and an overseer (*episkopos* in verse 7). The Bible authors use both terms when writing about leaders in the church, and here Paul appears to use them interchangeably.

LESSON 3: TRUTH, PURITY, AND CHRIST ALONE

Crete was a place of ungodly behavior. To follow Christ in such a place would require behaving in ways that were different from the norm—as it does in most places—and all the social alienation and other rejection that sometimes comes from living differently. Sadly, it appears the church community offered little support. Instead of finding a respite from the culture of lies, believers also found lies and evil-minded deception within the church itself. Trying to escape the pressures to be worldly found all over Crete, in the church they found themselves faced with pressure to be religiously snobby—which is no better.

Ironically, the false teachers who were preaching separateness and purity were actually offering another version of defilement and evil. They appear just as inclined to be liars as were any other Cretans. This is no surprise, since self-effort and a prove-yourself-to-God attitude actually have no power to produce true holiness. Paul writes about the futility of man-made religious regulations in Colossians 2:23. "Although these have a reputation for wisdom by promoting self-made religion, false humility, and severe treatment of the body, they are not of any value in curbing self-indulgence."

The passage shows that self-based effort to be religiously pure not only fails to work but also produces new evils: We defile our minds when we add human rules to God's law or trust human effort above faith in God. We scar our consciences when we tell ourselves that our devotion to doable, human regulations has made us pure before a holy God. We lie to the world when we claim to know God but actually trust ourselves and our "superiority." And we are unfit for the work of advancing Christ's kingdom when we fail to live out the gospel that says true righteousness is found only in him.

There actually is a great mission opportunity on Crete if only the churches will preach and live out the true gospel. The message that Christ has died for sin to make us dearly-loved children of God, and has risen in power and reigns from heaven, should be welcome relief from both the lie-to-get-ahead culture on Crete and the smug-regulations culture in the church. Titus has good news to share with all.

LESSON 4: TRUTH AND GODLY LIVING

Although it might be tempting to focus on the differences between the instructions given to each group mentioned in Titus 2, we learn more about godly living when we look at the similarities. Paul does not seem to be mandating different roles, but rather to be applying the same gospel principles to a number of roles that already exist on Crete. Everyone, regardless of their situation (and some were surely unhappy with their lot in life), could still adorn the gospel. For example, the members of every group should be concerned to act in ways that bring respect to themselves and to God. They should put concern for others ahead of their personal desires. They should be in control of their behavior. They should be careful about their speech. They should be concerned for decency. And they should care about their part in the pattern of gospel growth where one believer demonstrates to another how to live for Christ. All of this is also good teaching for us today, regardless of our station in life.

This instruction should remind us that *how* we go about the daily tasks of life is more important than *what* we do in life. Even the smallest tasks can be performed with faithfulness, concern for others, encouraging speech, etc.—so that the gospel is adorned in everything.

EXERCISE: Be careful not to let the exercise become an opportunity for trying to churn up more self-effort or greater self-fed faith. The strength of our faith is not the issue, as even a small amount of faith can move a mountain (Matthew 17:20). The point is *to whom* we look—to Jesus! Christian growth comes through faith in the promises of the gospel, and even that faith is received from God as a gift (Ephesians 2:8). So to grow, we must seek God and receive help from him. You may need to counsel participants on how to seek God and how to be open to receiving from him. The traditional "means of grace" are a good place to start: We seek God and receive grace from him through prayer. We also seek God and receive help from him through his Word—for example, by reading the Bible, meditating on the promises of Scripture, listening to the preached word, and experiencing the word in the Lord's Supper. Make sure participants understand that these should be means to seek God in weakness and need, not ways to coerce God by proving our religious devotion.

LESSON 5: TRUTH AND GOD'S GRACE

The grace of the gospel changes how we live in countless ways. Many of the main ways will be brought out in this lesson's article and exercise, but the group will probably be able to think of some of them on its own during the initial Bible conversation. Some chief possibilities:

❏ The good news that Jesus will return teaches us to live with expectation, patience, awareness of coming judgment, and hope for ourselves and the world.

❏ The good news that Jesus gave himself to redeem us teaches us to live free of shame and guilt, to respond to his love with grateful love for him and others, and to lay down our own lives as well.

❏ The good news that we are Jesus's own possession teaches us to serve God with an heir's devotion rather than in slavish fear, and to realize that we are able to resist temptation because the devil no longer owns us.

❏ The good news that we are cleansed and made eager to do good works teaches us to serve God with confidence, and to go out on mission.

❏ And the fact that all of this is God's grace, not earned by us, teaches us to live humbly and to work on our obedience in a way that constantly seeks God's help.

We might be tempted to neglect any of these teachings: Some of us live with little daily anticipation of the world to come. Others downplay the redeeming sacrifice of Jesus. We might prefer to be sluggish about the hard work of obedience, or we miss the joy of being brought into God's family. We might acknowledge grace in principle but still give in to a slavish sense that we must earn God's mercy. All of these (very common) struggles tend to stop us in our tracks when it comes to zealously serving God, because they eat away at our motivation. They also dampen the sense of joy and missional urgency behind Paul's announcement that "the grace of God has appeared, bringing salvation for all people." It's good to regularly turn to gospel-rich passages like this one because, as verse 12 says, God's grace teaches us "to deny godlessness and worldly lusts and to live in a sensible, righteous, and godly way in the present age."

LESSON 6: TRUTH AND DEVOTION

As verse 3 mentions, the desire to build ourselves up and put others down comes naturally to sinful human beings. Because of this, the godly character described in verses 1–2 ought to make believers stand out in any community. Others might at first find it hard to understand, or might suspect our motives, but consistently selfless living should eventually attract many of them to Jesus. "By this everyone will know that you are my disciples, if you love one another" (John 13:35).

We can become so used to hearing the truths of the gospel that we lose the wonder they bring. Without the gospel, the selfish lifestyle described in verse 3, where we are stuck knowing nothing else but to live for our own passions while disregarding others, becomes the accepted norm. The gospel is a striking change first of all because it introduces a completely different way—the way of kindness that flows from God's startling kindness to us. With this comes other good news that likewise changes everything: the pressure to earn honor and success is replaced by the grace of receiving freely from God, the futility of trying to be a better person is replaced by the transforming power of the Spirit, and the sad certainty of death is replaced by eternal life.

These gospel truths continue to transform us throughout our lives in this world. We must be reassured of them again and again or we will tend to revert back to our old way of life. We will not feel free to be kind and gentle toward others unless we know that Christ has removed the pressure to earn honor and success for ourselves. We will give up trying to be a better person unless we know that this is God's powerful work in us and his promise for us. And we will selfishly, fearfully amass worldly things for ourselves unless we know that eternal life awaits us with its far greater treasures.

LESSON 7: TRUTH AND HUMILITY

Those who devote themselves to gospel teaching also devote themselves to good works. In contrast, the people engaged in debates about lesser matters seem to have little interest in doing good works. They are not merely debating theology, but are quarrelsome and divisive. They *enjoy* arguments and conflict, and would rather stir up a juicy controversy than spend a day meeting someone's needs. Even after being corrected, they won't give up their argument. This shows that arguing itself means more to them than the point they are defending. They are not teachable, and this lack of humility is a clear sin. It condemns such people regardless of what points they are making.

It also sounds likely that those stirring up quarrels had a mind-set of superiority that denied the grace of the gospel. We don't know what exactly they were asserting about genealogies and the law, but the mention of those two items suggests they may have bought into the false teaching confronted earlier in the letter, so that these people considered themselves superior Christians because of their Jewish heritage or because they kept certain aspects of the Jewish ceremonial laws. Such teaching denies the sufficiency of Christ and the truth that we are all equally needy outside of him and blessed only in him. Of course, it is good to advocate rigorous obedience to God. But whatever these people were advocating, they went beyond God's actual requirements and did so with an attitude of superiority and a desire to win arguments. Rigorous gospel obedience ought to be humble, not looking to rank oneself above others on the basis of superior understanding or devotion.

Based on these observations, we might put up some fences around our own theological debates. Healthy and rigorous discussion can be helpful, but those who participate should be teachable. Many of us can relate to finding more pleasure in arguing than in doing good to others, or more pleasure in winning an argument than in learning the truth. We must guard against such attitudes.

Certainly, we must prioritize our agreement about the gospel ahead of our disagreements about lesser matters. But more than that, we must prioritize our *gospel attitude*: we must be willing to be corrected if wrong and resist feeling superior when we are right. Such an attitude creates a great environment for truly helpful discussions about God and how to be godly.

On the matter of missionaries, Apollos is mentioned in both Acts and 1 Corinthians as a companion of Paul who helped spread the gospel and traveled, as Paul and Titus did, across the Aegean Sea adjacent to Crete. It is likely that he and Zenas were stopping in Crete along the way on some sort of missionary endeavor. Paul says Titus and the church on Crete should be diligent in how they help these missionaries, taking care to really meet their needs rather than just going through the motions, so that they will lack nothing. Paul's words indicate both generosity and intimate involvement, not disinterested help from a distance. This passage suggests missionaries ought not to be scraping by, as if weak support from the church were one of their sufferings for Christ. Rather, they should feel amply supported and well appreciated, especially when their needs are urgent. In this way, both they and the believers who send them will be fruitful.

In verse 14, Paul may still have the traveling missionaries in mind as he writes about being devoted to good works that address pressing needs, or perhaps the needs of Zenas and Apollos caused Paul to think about how believers ought to meet each other's needs in all situations. In either case, we should be involved enough in each other's lives that we know each other's needs and are quick to meet them, as happens within families. We might ask ourselves: Do we know the pressing needs of the missionaries we support? How will we find out what those needs are? How will the gospel encourage us to respond?